INSPIRATION: A User's Guide

By Gill Woon

Paperback ISBN 9781907685798

ePub ISBN 9781907685804

Mobipocket/Kindle ISBN 9781907685811

Published in the UK by MX Publishing
335 Princess Park Manor, Royal Drive, London, N11 3GX
www.mxpublishing.co.uk

Cover design by
www.staunch.com

CONTENTS

Your guide

Caminante, son tus huellas
El camino, y nada mas
Caminante, no hay camino
se hace camino al andar
Al andar se hace camino,
y al volver la vista atras
Se ve la senda que nunca
Se ha de volver a pisar.
Caminante, no hay camino
Sino estelas en la mar

Wayfarer, your footsteps make the road
And nothing else
Wayfarer, there is no road
You make the road as you go
You make the road as you go
And as you look behind,
You can see the track that you
Will never tread again.
Wayfarer, there is no road
Only foam-trails in the sea.

Antonio Machado, Proverbs and Songs

I have always been fascinated by inspiration - what it is, how it works, and the strange and mysterious way that it appears to come and go, however much those of us who are seeking it wish to hold on to it. Like a wave on the beach, it creeps in across the sand, suddenly overwhelming us with its irresistible power, then just as quickly it's gone, and we are left invigorated but unable to catch it or stop its progress. Or like a soft breeze, so welcome and refreshing on a hot day, it comes as if out of nowhere, to gently caress, and then, just as gently, it is gone.

I'm not the only one who has experienced this. People have been wondering about, been frustrated by, thought about, talked about, written about, searched for, and often found, this elusive quality certainly for as far back as written records exist (and probably even before that). There seems to be an inexhaustible craving for it - even in our supposedly cynical and sophisticated 21st Century.

'Tell me, where is Fancy bred - or in the heart, or in the head?'

Shakespeare: The Merchant of Venice

'Rarely, rarely comest thou, Spirit of Delight'

Shelley: Rarely, rarely, comest thou

'Many of us wish we were more creative. Many of us sense we are more creative, but unable to tap that creativity. …We hunger for what might be called creative living '

Julia Cameron: 'The Artist's Way'

Because of the mysterious way inspiration behaves - seeming to 'just happen', or 'descend' out of nowhere, apparently unsought by us, many people believe that it is somehow 'god-given' (even if they don't personally believe in a god), and cannot therefore be easily achieved or held on to for very long; that it is out of our control (like the waves on the beach or the breeze I described earlier). They believe that it must 'belong' in some way to the exalted realm of the 'true artist', so if they are not a writer, poet, painter, sculptor or doing something 'creative', inspiration is not really for them.

So they discount or overlook any feelings they may genuinely experience of being 'in the flow', having great ideas and insights, or achieving wonderful things, as some kind of accident, not really the product of true inspiration but as lucky chance, or perhaps coming from *someone else's* inspiration which has somehow rubbed off on them. Yet the word 'inspiration' itself actually also means 'breathing in', - that is to say, inspiration is as natural and human a state as breathing! Whoever heard of anyone saying 'Who, me! I never breathe - it's only for those people over there, the 'inspired ones"?

Well, I am here to tell you that this belief - that inspiration is just for the chosen few - is nonsense. - I am on a one-woman mission to nail the pernicious myth that only poets, writers, painters and others in the 'creative' fields are able to be, likely to be, or, worse, are entitled to be, 'inspired'.

While I'm about it I'd also like to nail the corollary of this belief - that inspiration cannot be 'drawn down' - that we have to wait about for the Muse to visit us on a whim. We can access it if we seek it in the right ways. While we cannot all be a Leonardo da Vinci or a Dickens, inspiration is free, accessible to and, what is more, waiting to be explored by anyone and everyone who is ready and open to the experience.

"Soul loves the journey itself. The textures and undulations of the path it has made through the landscape by hazard and design, are nourishing in themselves. '

(David Whyte, 'The Heart aroused: poetry and the preservation of the soul in Corporate America')

I decided to write this guide to inspiration not because I claim to be an expert on the topic - but to share my own insights as a fellow-traveller on this journey. I chose the metaphor of the journey because it is shared by people from many different cultures and backgrounds, and because it mirrors in many ways, as I will show, the individual's experience of searching for, finding, using and learning from inspiration. It also lifts from us the burden of expectation - after all, if you decide to visit somewhere new for the first time, you would not expect to know everything about it or to be an expert about it, would you? You would never travel anywhere new if you had this expectation before you set out!! Even after many visits you may still be learning more. This, as seasoned travellers will testify, is part of the excitement and fun of real travel - it's tremendously liberating to learn that it is OK not to know everything but just to step out in faith that we will learn as we go along.

That said, it *is* a good idea to find out as much about the place, and prepare yourself for the visit as best you can, before you go. This is why, in 'Inspiration: a user's guide' I have included chapters on how to prepare, what to take along with you, how to overcome setbacks you may encounter on the way, who can help and how to find them. Because I believe it's good to learn from people who have been there and got the t-shirt as well, I've also included a number of personal anecdotes, hints and tips from inspired people from all backgrounds, walks of life and professions, known and less well known. They include Shaun Wallace, first Black 'Mastermind' winner, Mike Southon, well-known entrepreneur and author, Nick Williams, a motivational speaker and writer on entrepreneurship with heart, and Trevor Baylis OBE, inventor of the clockwork radio.

So, if you are looking for inspiration in work, life, relationships, career etc. join me on the journey. If you believe, like me, that inspiration is not the exclusive preserve of an inspired elite; if you are prepared, to step up, accept the challenge and put in a little time and effort, then join me on the journey.

A little about the person behind this book

I am not an all-round travel expert! But I do love travel, believe it can be a powerful means of learning and developing people, and that it is everyone's birthright to find and bring as much inspiration as possible into their lives.

Like many people, I've always said 'One day, I will write a book'. But, also like many others, while I liked the idea, the *reality* was somehow a lot harder to handle. There always seemed to be something more 'important' and pressing to be done in my day-to-day life. My gremlins also got at me, telling me 'Who are you to write a book? You'll never write as good a book as so-and-so..'and so on, and so on. So what changed?

As an NLP Practitioner and trainer, coach and therapist for people with learning disabilities, I am fascinated by how people learn and grow as individuals, and specifically why it is that learning is such a joy, and so life-enhancing for some, while signalling frustration, boredom, and embarrassment and feelings of failure for others.

Through my work with a variety of learners, I've come to gain a greater understanding of the wonderful, almost magical way the human brain can and does work at the top of its potential. It's as if we are surrounded by hundreds of tons of buried gold, some of which might, sadly, never be discovered because we are looking in the wrong place or digging with the wrong tools.

During my career, I've had the privilege of working with many people with specific learning disabilities (dyslexia, dyspraxia, ADD - Attention Deficit Disorder - and so on). My experience with these people has shown me how, even when the odds appear to be stacked against some human beings, they are capable of making the most inspiring and amazing efforts to improve their chances in life. I've been able to witness the joy of people, who thought they could never achieve their cherished goals, achieve them through their own efforts and with the support of others. It's helped me to understand how everyone needs a trigger to stimulate them into action - could be something small or large, but once activated, off they go, and there's no stopping them!

Seeing this has acted as a trigger to me to write this book. Inspiration leads to action. The secret is to keep looking for the trigger, and being ready to take action - to set off on the journey - when you find it.

I hope that this book will act as a trigger for some of you out there who are looking right now.

Why this journey matters

Here is my manifesto. I believe, passionately, that inspiration is not just for the inspired elite. It is possible for just about anyone, no matter what their occupation, interests, background, race, religion, education, gender etc. to start and finish this journey triumphantly, if they reflect on, and follow, some of the ideas and examples in this book, or use them as a springboard for their own ideas.

Furthermore, inspiration is not just an 'added extra', which the human race can survive without. It is and has always been essential to our survival as a species, and is indispensable for the future of any kind of humanity worthy of the name. When we believe - or settle for thinking - that we can live without inspiration, we are betraying our essential humanity; we are not truly 'living' .Using our imaginations, acting on them; creativity - these are what make us human.

*'We can certainly now assert that at least a reasonable, theoretical and empirical case has been made for the presence within the human being of a tendency toward, or **need for** growing in a direction that can be summarised in general as Self-actualisation, or psychological health, ...he has*

within him a pressure towards unity of personality, toward **spontaneous expressiveness**, *toward full Individuality and identity....**toward being creative**....The human being is so constructed that he presses toward fuller and fuller being,,,,*
Robert Hartman: 'The Science of Value'

As far back as 1943, the psychologist, Abraham Maslow, proposed in his 'Theory of Human Motivation' that individuals have a hierarchy of needs, represented as a pyramid (see diagram below):

MASLOW'S HEIRARCHY OF NEEDS

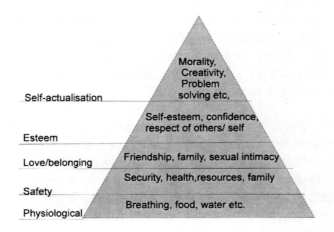

The pyramid shows five levels of need which are

broadly grouped into 'physiological' (what you need to keep you alive) and 'growth needs' (what you need to make you fully human). Once the basic, physiological needs (food, air, water, safety etc) are met, at some point people will feel driven to pursue the higher, or growth, needs. The topmost need is 'self-actualisation', which includes creativity, spontaneity and problem-solving (characteristics associated with inspiration).

Maslow described this as *'what a man can be, he must be'*. Humans have an instinctive need to make the most of their abilities and to strive to be the best they can be. Once their basic needs are satisfied, people will therefore have a need, almost a hunger, to be inspired. Of course, they may not recognise this - hence, I believe, the feelings of dissatisfaction and lack of purpose among many in our materially wealthy Western society who are comparatively well fed, housed and safe; hence the search for 'something more' among many who are wondering 'what life is about'.

These people are, I believe, looking for something to inspire them. This might also explain why some people living in conditions which we might describe as ''deprived' (for example, in some countries in the developing world) can demonstrate joy and generosity of spirit and a kind of fullness of life which in some ways our communities lack.

There's more. Scientists are discovering more and more all the time about how the amazing human brain works. It appears that our brains are *programmed* to be creative; to search for inspiration and to find meaning in our lives and the world around us. The brain works by building up patterns of response over time - that is how we learn effectively (see the 'Learning Ladder' model in Chapter 5) but is also capable of, and does, literally, *grow* in response to certain stimulating experiences, the brain cells, or neurons, growing larger and making new neural connections.

Furthermore, although we are born with massive potential, much of the actual development of the brain takes place after birth, in the outside world. Experience 'conditions' the brain - so you could say that the brain *needs to be* stimulated to develop to its full potential. It therefore also follows that our brains are in this respect largely our own creation, and it is therefore up to *us* to stimulate them
as fully as possible. (Source: 'The Amazing Brain', Evan Ornstein).

It has been known for some time that the two main cerebral hemispheres or halves of the main part of the brain are associated with, and direct, very different activities.

 Broadly speaking, the left side of the brain is responsible for language, logic, numbers, analysis and sequencing. The right hemisphere, often called the 'creative' side of the brain, deals with rhythm, spatial awareness, colour, imagination and dimension. Each side of the brain controls its opposite side of the body and they are linked by a network of neurons. It appears that for most people one side of the brain is dominant, and for centuries in our Western culture it is the left, logical, side that has been more greatly prized by society.

'Logic brain is our brain of choice in the Western Hemisphere...logic brain was and is our survival brain. ..anything unknown is perceived as wrong and possibly dangerous...logic brain is the brain we usually listen to, especially when we are telling ourselves to be sensible...'

(Julia Cameron, 'The Artist's Way')

Experiments with very young children have shown that, before entering school, most of them rank as predominantly 'right brain'. Our education system currently places a higher premium on mathematics, logic and language (predominantly 'left-brain' skills) than on drawing, painting or using the imagination, and only 10% of these same children will typically rank as highly creative by the time they are 7 years old - while by adulthood, high levels of creativity remain in only 2% of the population.

The neuroscientist and Nobel Prize Winner Roger Sperry, writing about this in the Seventies, had this to say:

' there appear to be two modes of thinking, verbal and nonverbal, represented rather separately in left and right hemispheres respectively, and ...our modern education system, as well as science in general, tends to neglect the nonverbal forms of intellect. What it comes down to is that modern society discriminates against the right hemisphere'

It seems as if this might, however, be changing as communities and individuals realise that we actually need to use *both* sides of our brains actively to benefit society and ourselves.

However, the skills and potential our brains have not been using do not 'disappear'. The brain is amazingly plastic (tests on recovery of stroke and severe accident victims have testified to its ability to compensate for lost skills) and can be trained to rediscover its 'lost' right-sided playfulness and ability to dream and envisage possibilities.

It follows that it is not only 'right sided' ie 'creative' individuals who can be inspired or inspirational. For one thing, we can all get in touch with our 'right sidedness' even if we are in the habit of accessing and using the left hemisphere in daily life. In effect, we can ourselves harness and direct this process - we can control, rather than be in the control of, our brain's processes.

The key to finding and harnessing inspiration, then, is learning how your brain works, being aware of your thinking 'habits' and getting into a new habit, of making *new* neural connections by by-passing the old patterns to search for new ones, by associating different (and apparently unconnected) thoughts and ideas, and overriding your internal 'censor' (your left brain) to make the most of them.

For another, as I will show later in this book, Inspiration comes in many forms and can be interpreted and worked out in many ways. It is for us to learn as much as possible about ourselves, how our own amazing brains work, and to use them in the way which best suits us. And we may have great ideas, but if we do not put them out in the world through planning and design, collaboration and action, they stay just that - great ideas and no more.

We need our whole brains - left and right side - to bring our great ideas to fruition.

Whether we are left or right brained, It's certainly true that right now our world needs inspired people, or people who believe they can become inspired, just as much as it ever did (some might say more, but I refuse to be such a pessimist!). It's been said before, but I shall say it again - we live in a time of constant, ever-faster, change and upheaval, where the old certainties of life are being increasingly challenged. According to recent statistics, 15% of students in the UK leave full-time education at 16 - where they have spent 10 or more years of their lives - still unable to read or write.

Approximately 10 % of the world's population controls 90 % of the world's resources (Source: ghanaweb.com). Many people feel tired, despairing, lacking or empty, or see threat rather than challenge in new technologies or approaches which appear to sideline their hard-won skills without offering a positive alternative. Others feel like passive observers of their own lives, rather than active participants, and need to be empowered, engaged, in short - inspired. When wars and disasters happen, it is all too easy to lose heart and feel as if we cannot influence events. But, if we look more carefully, we can see many examples of how individuals and groups have bucked the trend and brought about change for the better in all sorts of inspired ways.

When an individual, or a group, follows through on inspired ideas, harnessing the skills and abilities they have to galvanise themselves and others, they can make a big difference. I'm thinking of the examples of Rosa Parks (a very 'ordinary' woman whose simple, but extraordinary, action in refusing to sit at the back of a bus was one of the key triggers for the Civil Rights movement in the USA), of Camilla Batmangelidh, whose 'Kids Company' has saved the lives and hopes of many young people in London, and many, many others. What are the odds that some people said to these inspired ones something along the lines of 'Why bother, you won't make a lot of difference...'but they went ahead and did it anyway. '.

Perhaps the question, then, should be, not why do we need inspiration, but 'How can we do without it?' What happens when people are *not* inspired, or are motivated by something other than true inspiration to take action? You could argue that those who seek to impose their narrow view of the world on others for ideological reasons, and use violent means to do so, are, like the inspirational individuals I interviewed for this book and many others, seeking meaning, to make some sense of their world, think they have found an explanation, make up their minds to take action, and follow through. Are they also 'inspired'?

I believe that the answer probably lies in the outcome. Maslow doesn't examine this, but true inspiration comes from a good place (God, or if you prefer, the Universe or a presiding spirit) and brings only good to the inspired individual and to others, never harm. It is 'contagious' in the best sense of the word - others follow the example set and spread the good around. It opens up new possibilities and brings a little (or even a lot) more light and joy into the lives of everyone touched by it. And once you start getting involved with true inspiration, it is an unstoppable force in your and others' lives. I would be honoured and very happy if this book made its own small contribution to spreading the 'inspiration bug' just a little bit further.

What does inspiration mean to you? What should the traveller be looking out for?

The word, 'Inspiration' is related to the word 'spirit' and also to the word for breath'. So, when you are breathing and keeping yourself alive, you are literally, inspiring - breathing in the air that nourishes you. Inspiration is as vital to spiritual life as air is to physical life - and we can all be inspired, just as we can all breathe. Although people's experiences of inspiration may differ, there are some fundamental similarities to look out for - here are some pointers:

Have you ever felt 'in the flow' as if everything is going together, and going your way, when you were working on a project or a piece of work, or a hobby, which you truly loved and enjoyed, and were exhilarated by? You felt challenged by it , but at the same time confident that you could meet the challenge even though it stretched you? This is what some people call 'being in the Zone',. and was familiar to Leonardo da Vinci as 'Dimostrazione' (Demonstration)- one of the seven concepts he devised to explain how he achieved his phenomenal artistic and scientific discoveries. *(See Michael Gelb's book 'How to think like Leonardo da Vinci').*

Have you ever felt truly at home with something or with a group of people, as if this is what you were meant to be doing and where you were meant to be doing it? I believe that in those moments you were inspired..

- You will come to know when you are, and when you are not, inspired.

'A man should learn to detect and watch that gleam of light which flashes across his mind from within' *(Ralph Waldo Emerson)*

- *'one must set oneself to watch for and cultivate certain fragile moods of the heart. One should..recognise it as an important messenger and listen to its message..'* *(Paul Brunton, 'Search for the Overself')*

Learn to recognise this in yourself and attune yourself to the state of being inspired. Look out for the signals.

As with many things worth doing, practice makes perfect. You will make some mistakes (that is how we learn) but you will find that, if you trust, you will be increasingly able to detect inspiration in yourself.

- People who are inspired use positive words like 'passion' (we will keep coming back to this one)'love', 'energy', enthusiasm' (incidentally, 'enthusiasm' means literally 'filled with God'). The word Inspiration itself means 'filled with the spirit'.

-   Inspiration leads to positive outcomes or actions of some kind (small or large). It leads to growth and development in the inspired one (and in those touched by them. Inspiration is 'contagious' in the best sense of the word).

As the poet and playwright Federico Garcia Lorca said:

'it .. is a power and not a behaviour, it is a struggle and not a concept'

- It feels good all or most of the time! Exciting, truly alive, swept along, 'possessed' - though it might also be a bumpy ride some of the time if it takes you outside your comfort zone, as inspiration often tends to do). For some it means heightened sensory awareness - colours are brighter, sounds sweeter. It's a bit like being in love!

'the creative person..is all there, totally immersed, fascinated, absorbed in the present..utterly lost'
(Abraham Maslow)

When people are inspired, they feel 'in the flow' - everything seems to come together, and connections are made that might not otherwise be made, giving a sense of a greater whole, attuned to the one end. Life seems to make more sense than it sometimes does. They don't notice the passing of time and they are never bored.

There is a feeling of rightness and completeness about inspired activities or projects.

- People often experience 'serendipity' when they are inspired - the little fortunate, seemingly miraculous, coincidences that come together to move a project along (not

    – always exactly when we expect them, or even
    in the form we expect, but they will come).

In fact, one of the joys of this journey is looking out for the 'surprise bonuses' along the way. Goethe describes this phenomenon as

'a whole stream of events..raising in one's favour all manner of unforeseen incidents and meetings and material assistance which no man could have dreamt would come his way'.

At certain times, while writing this book, I found the 'right' quotations or others came up with suggestions for interviewees, or helped facilitate them for me. If you are involved in or embarking on a long term project, I would recommend that you look out for these - they can keep you going when you sometimes feel as if you have lost your way.

- People feel as if they are moving forwards, towards a bigger goal or objective or are in a project that is right for them, or being turned away from or blocked from one that is not right for them. As Paul Brunton put it:

'inspiration carries with it the inspiring sense, the positive certainty of the success or rightness towards which it is leading',

Try this out:

Take a few moments to think about those times when **you** felt 'in the flow' or inspired, and what characterised them.

What were you doing? Who was there?

Where was it? Did they have anything in common?

What brought it about, and what ended it?

(Jot your thoughts down here.....)

Getting ready for the journey

All good guide books start out by telling you what you need to take on your journey, how best to prepare, and this one is no exception!

I'm sure you'll have read the advice from travel experts which runs something like: 'take half the clothes you think you need, but twice the money'? Well, the advice I am going to give is a little like that. You do not need to take loads of luggage with you on this trip - in fact, the lighter the better. But you do need to do a little bit of work on yourself before you go.

To help you do this, I've put together a questionnaire for you to do. It will help you to focus on some of the areas you need to think about as you go along, and that we will be looking at in this book. Don't worry if you haven't experienced some of these things or are unsure - you don't need to get it 100% 'right' before you start - in fact there is no such thing as 100% right in this kind of exercise. It's intended to start you thinking about what actions you want to take and what is important for you. This journey is not a day trip but a life time's adventure you are now booked in on. This questionnaire will help you to set the scene.

HOW INSPIRED ARE YOU?

Anyone can be inspired - but where are you right now? This questionnaire should help you find out. Answer the questions as honestly as you can, but don't spend too long agonising over them - first impressions are usually best.

- Do you have a real enthusiasm or passion for something?   Y/N

- If the answer to Q1 was 'Yes', can you say what it is that makes you enthusiastic or passionate about it?

  (jot down as notes, bullets, pictures - whatever works best for you)

- If the answer to Q1 was 'No', can you think back to a time when you did feel enthusiastic about something? jot down what that was here, and when you felt like this

- When you were a child, what did you want to do 'when you grew up'? (honest answers here, doesn't matter how wacky they seem - this is for your eyes only)

- If you're employed at the moment, how do you feel about the job you do on a scale of 1-10 (1 being 'I'd rather be anywhere else' and 10 being 'I couldn't be happier')

- If you are not employed, what job/work/occupation would you really love to do. Ignore qualifications, age, gender, fitness levels and other considerations - it's fantasy time! Maybe you've always had a 'secret ambition'? If so, put it down here.

- Is there a place you've always wanted to visit - and what makes you want to go there?

- Who is the person - living, dead, fictional, real - you most admire?

- What is it about this person that makes you admire them?

- Can you say when you last took a risk (doesn't have to be physical, doesn't have to be major eg running off to sea!)

- What motivated you to do that? What was the outcome, and how did you feel about it?

- Do you try new things (eg new foods, visiting different places, different experiences, meeting different people, etc)

- How often?

- Do you reflect on your own feelings, emotions and reactions to events and other people?

- Do you capture them, eg in a diary, scrapbook etc.

- Think about your friends and acquaintances. How do you really feel about them? Is there an 'inner group', are there people you feel more comfortable with, how much do you feel you can be yourself or reveal to them? When you're with a group, do you tend to do the same things - do you ever suggest doing something to the group? Who is the leader of the group?

I hope this has started you thinking about and reflecting on yourself and how you tend to react to things around you and behave.

There aren't any definitive right or wrong answers - the point of the exercise is to start looking at yourself and seeing what you are happy with and what you could change - because that is where our journey begins.

How did you fare? Don't worry if you found there were some areas that were new to you or where you feel you still need to do some work - don't let that stop you - you can start right now, from where you are. Just be mindful of them as you go along. If I were to recommend any important pieces of 'luggage' to take with you on this journey, it would be an open mind and a receptive heart

The first point is to be clear about **where you are heading**. When you go on holiday, you book to go to a particular destination, which you have chosen for a particular reason (the climate, the scenery, it's suitable for children, etc). you don't usually wait till you get to the airport and then pick out where you are going on the map with a pin!

So the first point to be made is: **BE CLEAR OF YOUR DESTINATION**.

Guides to goal-setting (or map-reading for that matter) always stress this, and it is crucial. Part of the reason is that your subconscious mind will do what your conscious brain tells it to do, and if you create a game-plan 'in your mind' then it will be far easier for the brain to follow through and create it in reality. You need a map or plan to undertake any successful journey or enterprise. This does not have to be in exhaustive detail - but you do need a good idea of where you are going. You also need to be aware of:

•   How long you think it might take - although you might need to revisit your plan and should do so regularly to see whether you are keeping to this and if not, why not (there might be a very good reason)

- What resources you might need along the way (people, equipment, money, learning etc)

- What impact your journey might have on others around you - it's always a good idea to keep loved and trusted ones informed about where you plan to go, and enlist their support (but watch out for those who might sabotage you - see some tips for dealing with them later in 'Problems and Pitfalls')

- How you are going to keep yourself nourished along the way (to remind you why you started and keep you going and on track).

- Last but not least, you should also have a 'contingency plan' to prepare for the unexpected! I have covered this in more detail later.

Meet (and learn from) some inspired travellers

A great way to learn about something and get new ideas and perspectives is to find out how people who have gone through an experience before us fared - what went well, or not so well, how they started and how they finished - whether we decide to follow their example, take from and adapt it, or reject it! That is why I've included the experiences of seasoned 'inspiration travellers' in a range of fields and from a range of backgrounds in this book. You will have heard of some of them but they all have equally important points to make about the inspiration journey. they have all been there, done that, and got the Inspiration t-shirt!

Perhaps the most interesting point about these people is that they are not resting on their laurels. For them, the journey is never really over - there's always something new and exciting to be discovered and learnt.

I asked my 'Inspired Travellers' these questions:

- **When/What time of day do you get inspiration?**

- **Are there any particular circumstances or situations which you find more inspiring than others (for example, do you need to be in a particular place/s, be alone or with others, to access inspiration?)**

- **Or does it just come, anytime, anyplace, anywhere?**

- **Can you get yourself into an inspired mood, or does it just happen (and you have to wait for it)?**

- **When you get inspired, does it come in the form of a picture, words, sounds, or omething else, or a combination of these?**

- **How do you capture ideas when they do come to you (eg., do you write them down in a notebook, draw a picture, record them, put them onto your PC or laptop, etc.)?**

These were the inspired (and inspiring) people I spoke to:

Nick Williams, author of *'The work we were born to do'*, former Director of Alternatives, a major venue for authors and workshop leaders, founder of the Heart at Work project, coach, and motivational speaker. Nick describes his own journey towards inspiration thus:

'Growing up, I did many of the things I was supposed to do and were socially acceptable - studied hard, got good qualifications,..worked hard, did well, became fairly successful, selling computers to Japanese banks....I was fairly happy to start with, but increasingly found it didn't hold much meaning for me. I ...began to ask myself some of the bigger questions like, 'Well, if I am not here to sell computers to banks, what am I here to do?'

By my late 20's, the disparity between my inner desires, dreams and longings and outer sense of self ..became so great that I could no longer contain that conflict. Out of that I made a decision to head in a new direction and ...made a break for authenticity rather than doing what I was supposed to. I crossed an invisible threshold and listened to the calling of my deeper self. I said to myself, 'I am going to follow my heart, my sense of joy and inspiration and see where it takes me.'

About inspiration, Nick said:

'I can be inspired any time of day, but mornings are often when I write. I get inspiration every time I sit down to write. I often get great ideas reading someone else's books, in conversation with my friend Barbara (Barbara Winter, author of *'Making a living without a job'*) talking to other friends, sometimes watching TV, listening to music or listening to a personal development CD. I am in the habit of immersing myself in inspiration every day.

Sometimes inspiration comes out of my own silence, and other times through some input that triggers something in me. I think I can get inspired anywhere, alone and with others. More than anything, I need to be away from negative people, although they often give me ideas too!

For me, inspiration is less about outer place, more about stimulation through ideas and insights. I can often get great ideas when I am sitting in the steam room at my gym after some exercise. My body relaxes and my mind expands.

Inspiration usually comes (to me) as words, ideas, a sense of alignment and quiet excitement and often it's 'Aha's' - feelings of recognition.

If I can, I immediately start writing on my PC or laptop, and if not I scribble thoughts down on pieces of paper, so that I remember them. However good or clear an idea, it can vanish quickly. '

Mike Southon, author of 'The Beermat Entrepreneur', entrepreneur and motivational speaker. Mike would be the first to say that his personal journey towards inspiration has been far from straightforward. Mike went to the same school as Richard Curtis and then on to public school where he met his now collaborator and lifelong friend, Chris West. While at school Mike was told 'You should go down to work the theatre.you'd enjoy it'. He believes that he has been in show business in one way or another ever since!

Mike went to Imperial College, London, to read Mechanical Engineering (he was thrown out after one year for preferring to drink beer and run after women..) then while working in lab jobs set up a Jazz Band with friends, which performed with great success at Oxford University events. Following this Mike finally took his degree in Chemical Engineering at Bradford University, then began working in the construction industry, graduated to selling scaffolding, then with friends got a sales job at UNIX, finally meeting the people who would help him set up the Beermat Entrepreneur Company - and the rest is history!

Themes running through his experience are: all experience is potentially valuable; the value of networking and making friends; flexibility and - persistence pays off in the end!

About inspiration, Mike said:

'Usually I think about problems and issues last thing at night – inspiration often happens subliminally. I often have the solutions by morning.

I work best in a small group with others, eg with 'Cornerstones' (Mike's group of people who spark creative ideas off each other and come up with practical solutions) in the pub!

It depends on the circumstances – I often get inspired reactively on clients' sites or in meetings when their problems are outlined.

I can get (myself) into an inspired mood – anyone who has appeared on stage knows how to turn this on – and off!

Usually inspiration comes to me as problem-solving patterns.

Of course, I note down inspirations on a beermat, but also like to explain ideas there and then, to a willing audience.

Yvonne Marie Batson Wright, poet, nurse and trainer, and coach. Yvonne has her own small company writing poetry 'to order' for special occasions. She realised she had this ability quite early on and decided to use it for her own satisfaction and an income, and to give others pleasure.

'My inspiration comes in the early hours of the morning – often when dawn is breaking and it is really quiet. I write and think best at this time. Six to eight am is also good – I write at my best when I have had a rest and have a clear mind.

Places also inspire me, such as the sea, waterfalls, big open spaces or green fields.

Sometimes travelling on the train or tube and watching people – their actions or expressions is also an inspiration. Just talking to people will also inspire..

If I am going through a challenging time this is a real inspiration to me to write, as it allows me to express how I feel. If a friend or colleague is going through tough times this can also be an inspiration. I am also inspired by positive events such as weddings or birthdays.

I can get myself into an inspired mood at any time and am sometimes called upon to write an immediate poem – I rise to the occasion!

My inspiration will come mainly from the spoken word, listening and hearing. I have however written poetry to match a picture.

I capture my ideas in note form in a book that I keep nearby. I also have a notebook in the car and a dictaphone recorder.

My husband Ian also inspires me. I admire his determination and drive, and have written for him many times. I am also inspired to write about members of my family who have touched my life.

Overall, I would say that I am always inspired to write as it is my passion – the poetry business means that I respond to orders and am inspired at that time for that specific event or person. '

Shaun Wallace, first Black winner of 'Mastermind', lecturer in Law and junior football coach. Shaun is a many-faceted and multi-talented character who is always looking out for the next challenge. Shaun has always been fascinated by history and Literature; as a child he always had his head in the Encyclopaedia.

Shaun found that he had a talent for learning, absorbing and remembering what he had learnt and this sparked his interest in quiz shows and particularly Mastermind, the king of quiz shows. He loved watching others compete but soon realised that he was able to answer as many questions as the winners, and began to enter quizzes himself, first locally, and then on TV, including '100%' and 'Fifteen to One', 'Greed' with Jerry Springer (he won £50,000 in 2001), the 'Waiting Game' with Ruby Wax, 'Brainteaser' on Channel 5, 'Nobody likes a Smartarse', and 'Beat the Nation' among others.

All this was, as Shaun saw it, good preparation for 'Mastermind'. When he saw a contestant win the show answering questions on sport, he realised that he stood a good chance of winning, and began to prepare - and at last, his dream, for which he had prepared so well, came true.

Shaun is still working as a Barrister, which was his ambition since he was 11 years old. He wrote to the Inner Temple, (they replied to his letter), and, as he says, the rest is history! Shaun also had a childhood ambition to be a footballer, inspired by Ossy Ardiles - he still coaches youth and acts as a mentor within the Black community.

So how did Shaun achieve all this? In his own words:

'When I pray at night, which I do at the same time no matter where I am or what I am doing, (it gives me) peace and solitude, and time to reflect.

I'm inspired by seeing people achieve things whether small or great, reaching their goals, no matter how big or small those are.

I can get myself into an inspired mood. (I'm also inspired) when I'm teaching others .

My philosophy is 'work hard, build your platform as high as you want to go….if you've got talent, it can be you' I have always daydreamed since childhood. I've always dreamed, for example, of being a lawyer, and of winning Mastermind!

And I've made my dreams come true.

The process of 'getting inspired' for me is something tangible. I see, feel and think inspiration. It becomes part of me.

Luisa Sanchez La Peña, sculptor and teacher/lecturer.

I asked Luisa how she came to be doing what she now does. She told me that it had been a long journey for her - a journey which began in Spain, her birthplace.

From the age of 7, every summer she used to visit a brick and tile factory which belonged to a friend's father. She recalls cycling there in the heat of the Spanish summer, and the discarded offcuts of red clay which lay about. Luisa loved the feel of the clay, and the workers used to allow her to mould shapes out of it, which she would then fire in the kiln. At this stage, Luisa's work was purely experimental - she had no teacher, just following her instinct. Later on her father encouraged her by teaching her to carve wood, and buying tools for her (bear in mind that this was rural Spain in the 60s where traditional attitudes to 'men's' and 'women's' work still held sway). He organised some lessons with a local carpenter but it didn't work out (Luisa still remembers the macho atmosphere in the carpenter's workshop where he and his friends would gather to smoke and talk politics - somehow a ten-year old girl didn't quite fit in).

Luisa's path led her away from making things with her hands - she qualified and practised as a doctor- but still had the hankering in her heart for the clay. She joined arts classes and read books about every aspect of handicrafts, biding her time.

Much later, when Luisa was married and had a young son, and had moved to England, she decided to enrol in an arts class locally 'to get some adult conversation'. She had meant to enrol in an upholstery class, but it was full.

Down the corridor was a sculpture class - somehow, it was meant to be!

So how does Luisa get inspired?

'(I can get inspired) Anytime, anyplace, anywhere!

I'm inspired when I'm working. It's been said: 'When the muse comes, she must find you working'

I'm always experimenting.

My work is based on the human body, so I spend a lot of time looking at people, for example, doing things like dancing.

When I'm inspired, I feel it physically. I get goose pimples, I notice it in my skin. Then I go straight for the clay. I experiment, eg turning things through 360 degrees to see what they look like.

Luisa described how she successfully completed a project dear to her heart, from the first germ of an idea through to the finished product. She saw a picture of a woman in a magazine and was struck by the curve made by the woman's back - unusual, and yet entirely natural. She found a model, and asked her to pose - the shape wasn't exactly the same, but it was near enough to act as a starting-point for Luisa's creative imagination. She made three small maquettes (small models) each ten inches tall, studied the lines of these until she found the curve she wanted to replicate. She was clear at this stage that she didn't want a fussy or distracting outline.

Moving on from this, Luisa experimented with a lifesize replica. It was hard work and she was impatient to get a result - several times the model broke and she had problems with her metal welder.

Finally she had a finished product which satisfied her - the whole process had taken four years. Luisa no longer has the statue - she was unable to store it, so decided to put it in her garden, where it disintegrated. She told me that she was happy with this as it returned to nature.

What did Luisa learn from this process? She told me that she learnt the value of seeing a project through from start to finish, but not taking it for granted and making no assumptions about where and how it would lead her - the piece evolved several times as she was creating it. She also learnt not to be too attached to outcome - the making and the learning were as important as the finished product. Lastly, she learnt the value of persistence and holding onto your dream despite difficulties.

Ray Cortis, musician, composer and organiser of inspired music-themed workshops for young people:

'Inspiration will come when you can accept it. It depends on your mindset at any given time, whether you are going to be inspired or inspirational (or both)

People with inspirational lives are good to have around, and I have found that they can turn on the inspirational tap within.

I usually write ideas down as a 'mind map' and then adapt them into work, love or family. '

Olive Hickmott, a health and wellness coach and author. Olive has a passion for helping people with chronic illness return to wellness, enabling children to achieve their potential through overcoming learning difficulties and supporting parents to grow too.

Olive trained as a mathematician and engineer and in corporate life she was an engineering director.

She describes how as a child and later, she struggled with lists of words to learn and had poor test results, and recalls never being able to read books for pleasure. It wasn't until much later, when Olive trained as a Neurolinguistic Programme Practitioner (NLP) that she found out the answer to her personal 'puzzle': a technique called 'Seeing Spells Achieving' which harnesses the power of visualisation to assist with spelling, reading, comprehension and memory. Olive works with children and adults with dyslexic tendencies to overcome their difficulties with learning.

Olive told me: ' About four or five years ago, I did a lot of work on myself, to find out what I wanted to do in life. I woke up and thought:'I'm going to be a health coach. I would describe myself as 'somewhat cavalier', because I don't worry too much about how I'm going to get to where I want to go; I am confident I will get there. For example, I learnt the 'Seeing Spells Achieving' technique one weekend and the next I walked into a Special Needs School and asked for their 'worst' two students to help. I take the view:

'What's the worst that could happen?'. When I learnt this technique, I immediately felt very strongly that it was the key to youngsters overcoming their spelling problems.

About a year after this, I was at a conference in the US and I asked 'how long is it till this is taught in our schools?' the answer I was given was 'no-one knows'. I didn't think that that was acceptable and you could say that that is what drives me on. I now have an even bigger goal: to stop dyslexia happening; if all primary school teachers knew and taught this technique, I firmly believe we could achieve that.

What time of day do you find most inspiring?

I'm at my best first thing in the morning; if I could get up at 5am every day I could achieve even more.

I get inspiration from following my life's purpose. I'm energised and motivated by doing the 'Big A' (Big Agenda) things.

If I'm in one-to-one coaching situations, or running a workshop, giving out new ideas, I feel inspired.

I was taught years ago that the Universe rewards action - and I believe it!

It comes in the form of energy - once energised I can do most things. I look at my rough notes, mull it over in my brain, get away from the computer and rough it out. I do use hemithink music which encourages left-right brain connection.

I often get 'too many' ideas; I journal which I find helps me to work a problem out or to clarify my thoughts.

Keith Hodgson, graphic designer, who has worked for, among others, the National Blood Donation Service. Keith has always known that he would pursue a career in visual art.

He studied this at College where he was presented with a number of options - he describes it as a process of elimination - he knew he would not be a Fine artist or a potter or go into fashion design, and 'gravitated' to graphic art. Keith's family background was in a number of creative fields, TV, film and architecture. At the time he was considering his career options, the British film industry was going through a low period and, as his brother worked at 'Harper's and Queen's' so a move into publishing seemed a good choice.

Keith worked for both large and small companies but prefers the latter 'because you can have more influence and I don't like bureaucracy'. Keith worked in the Maxwell organisation where he was the Creative Director of the publishing division, with 9 designers, 2 picture researchers and a studio manager working to him, and was in charge of 27 magazines - but he was happiest when he worked in a small outfit consisting of 6 creative people and was involved in everything.

The demise of Robert Maxwell acted as a trigger for Keith to make the decision about where he was happier working, and he now runs his own company.

Keith told me that:

'I get inspiration anytime, anyplace, anywhere. But I find that sitting, listening quietly to music and feeling relaxed helps. For me, the afternoon or evening are the best times. I find the seaside, the country, or open places inspiring.

Yes, I can get myself into an inspired mood! I'm inspired by music as I've said; I choose it for mood I want to create. Because my work is visual, I look at reference material, other designers' work, books and pictures. I mostly capture my ideas in pictures. It's a mix of quick sketches and sitting down straightaway and putting it into the computer. '

Here's how Keith approached a particular design project he undertook:

'As a practising graphic artist/designer, all my ideas have to have a commercial basis, and come out of an original brief from the client to solve the problem they have. This might be something as basic as a logo or identity for an individual, company, or event, or...getting information across to a target audience. ..could be anything from a simple letterhead, small leaflet, poster, newsletter, magazine or catalogue, or might end up being produced as a T-shirt, pen, sweet wrapper, mouse mat - anything that can carry a message and will be used by the target audience.

The ideas usually come from looking at reference material I have, graphic design manuals and books, art books or a library of samples I have collected. I then think about the problem for a while without putting anything on paper or screen, mulling it over until I think I'm ready to commit to set it out, using the computer design programmes (mostly).

The process can take minutes, hours or days. Sometimes you get it right immediately, sometimes it takes longer. '

I asked Keith how he overcomes barriers and setbacks during the process...

'Barriers are my own limitations in translating the idea through the design programme to give the result I want. Setbacks are predominantly a client who doesn't like the idea, so then I have to either start again or adapt, something you get used to doing as it goes with the territory.

There is often a great sense of achievement in creating and producing a piece of work for a client, as the work is produced in stages; when it's going well you get a buzz at each successfully completed stage and disappointment of varying levels when it doesn't go quite as you had planned. In the main I get a great deal of satisfaction as more often than not I do produce work that goes through without too many hiccoughs or set-backs, ...and anyway, you take those in your stride, they become another part of the problem to solve! '

Trevor Baylis, entrepreneur and inventor (of the Clockwork radio) who runs a website and training for would-be young inventors. Trevor was born in Kilburn, London, and spent his childhood in Southall. He was always an avid swimmer, and by the age of 15 was swimming competitively for Britain. At 16, Trevor joined the Soil Mechanics Laboratory in Southall and began studying mechanical and structural engineering at the local technical college.

At 20 Trevor began National Service as a physical training instructor, which gave him ample opportunity to swim for the Army. When he left the Army, he became a salesman for a Swimming pool company, later becoming involved in research and development and finally setting up his own company. He also worked as a stuntman on TV shows performing escape feats underwater! His other passion has always been inventing, particularly products to help physically handicapped people.

The story of the wind-up radio

In 1983, Trevor saw a TV programme about AIDs in Africa, which reported that in many regions radios were the only reliable means of communication, but that the need for batteries or electricity made them too expensive for most people. There was a need for a communications tool which did not rely on electricity or batteries. Hearing the word 'need' Trevor was inspired - as he says, 'Need is the catalyst for an inventor's 'raison d'etre' and immediately set about experimenting to find a solution to the problem. He found the a hand brace turning a motor would act as a generator to power the radio; the addition of a clockwork mechanism meant that a spring could be wound up and as this unwound the radio would play.

The first prototype ran for 14 minutes on a two minute wind. The clockwork radio was born!

As Trevor says:

'Chance favours the prepared mind' – inspiration comes any place and at any time.

Inspiration is pure chance; it cannot be forced. ..But it must be recognized and captured.

Inspiration usually comes to me in the form of pictures. Whether I write them down or not depends on whether they give me a 'buzz'.'

Harry Singha, founder of the Youth Coaching Academy, which develops young people in schools and youth organizations to coach their peers:

'I get inspiration from reminding myself of experiences (personal or otherwise) or making the impossible possible. I utilize my meditation periods (morning and tea time) to immerse myself with such experiences. I get inspiration from all forms of media and communication. The bigger the challenge for an individual or group, (the bigger the inspiration) is a factor.

No, I do not need to be in a particular place and am inspired when alone or with others. When someone/ a group is humble with their contribution, it inspires me. Witnessing young people and adults, breaking boards, jumping off telephone poles 40ft high and overcoming fears at our events would rate very high next to witnessing my own children demonstrating affection and unconditional love.

…inspiration comes anytime, anyplace, anywhere!

I can get myself into an inspired state whenever I choose. I simply ask myself a question to direct my focus to all the inspiration I have around me. I am blessed to be surrounded by amazing individuals at the Academy who are all role models of making a difference and each one is a source of inspiration.

…inspiration comes to me from songs, words, pictures, expressions, smells, tastes, stories and thoughts, a combination of all or separately. I have a drawer under my desk which stores all the stories of inspiration from the coaches and young people involved with the Academy.

I have a capture section in my journal/diary and I have been known to text people to remind me.'

Rebekah Renton, writer, editor and publisher of 'Be Unlimited' magazine (the first ever 'commercial' magazine focussing on self-development and spirituality and a pioneer in its field)

'Inspiration comes to me at any time, any place – that may sound a little like the Martini girl of the 80's! I think that the important thing is to always be open to new ideas and ways of thinking. Sometimes inspiration comes to me from the strangest of places; the uncomfortable meeting, the boring course or the frustrating relationship. The idea, here, is to turn a challenge into an opportunity.

I think it's the Chinese who use the same word for 'problem' as 'opportunity'. We have to learn how to be aware when our brains begin to shut down to the possibilities. For me, whenever I hear a negative voice in my head, I know I need to do something about my mental state. I know that I need to quieten the gremlins and look out for the idea or lesson. Inspiration is nothing to do with external influences, it has everything to do with how you choose to respond to the world and what is going on.

I choose (to get myself into an inspired mood) and then it happens.

Inspiration is feelings and ideas combined. It's exciting, coherent, and passionate. I always write my ideas down, where ever I can: scraps of paper, my hand, a note book, my computer....'

What can we learn from the Inspired travellers…

Inspiration is like a muscle…use it our lose it! Not seeking it out, avoiding it, or habitually ignoring it, causes it to weaken. At first, as with any exercise, it is effortful and hard to use some of the time, but with regular practice and exercise it becomes strong and effective.

If you are reading this, and agreeing with my words, thank you. If you are reading this, and thinking 'that doesn't sound like me', I'd like you to conduct a little fun experiment right now. Think of a hobby or pastime you really enjoy, or something you loved doing when you were younger, or a child. If you really cannot think of anything, ask a trusted friend or family member to help jog your memory. Now, find somewhere quiet and imagine yourself doing the hobby or pastime for a few moments (try to see or feel yourself doing it). How do you feel? Jot the words down, or draw a picture if you prefer, as they come to you.

Happy? Absorbed? Excited? You have recaptured a little of the flavour of joy and passion which children seem to find so natural and which we as adults so often lack, but which give life so much of its zest and flavour.

I would like everyone to experience far more zest and flavour in their lives! Think of the enthusiasm which Jamie Oliver brings to cooking, or Luciano Pavarotti to singing.

So what were the common themes in the experiences and practice of our inspired travellers?

- **Inspiration comes in many forms**

You'll have noticed that the people I interviewed were not all artists, poets, writers or painters (though some of them did come from these fields of endeavour). Their activities were varied, and so is the way they are inspired. If we could make one generalisation about inspiration drawn from their comments though, it might be 'Inspiration comes through the senses'. This is, after all, how we experience life. Perhaps not surprisingly, the interviewees working in visual fields experienced inspiration primarily through their sense of sight; others, working with music or dealing with people, through their hearing. Yet others talked about an almost tangible experience. Just to remind you:

'It comes as words or ideas' (Nick Williams)

'I feel it physically, on my skin – I get goose bumps' (Maria Luisa Sanchez La Peña)

..'problem solving patterns' (Mike Southon)

'(My inspiration comes) in pictures' (Trevor Baylis)

Here's a little test to find out which is your dominant sense. When you are experiencing something intense, or talking about it to someone else, listen to yourself, or ask that person to give you feedback on how you describe that experience. Do you, for example, say 'It looked fantastic', 'I didn't like the look of that', or do you commonly use expressions like 'It felt great', or 'I hear what you are saying'.

Which sense is most important to you – which one could you really not live without? It is likely that your inspiration will come through that sense.

- **Don't make assumptions about inspiration, or take it for granted**

Inspiration might not come in the way you expect it, or at the time you expect it to (even if you make a practice of seeking it, as you should) It's like the answer to a prayer – if you pray regularly your prayers will be answered – but while you will get what you *need*, you won't necessarily get everything you *wanted* or *thought* you wanted. You need to get clever at not only seeking out, but recognizing, inspiration.

That feeling that something is not quite right? The nagging sensation that 'more could be done' or 'it could be better'? That something is missing and you need to go the extra mile? That could be inspiration tugging at your coat-sleeve, calling for your attention.

Some people are inspired by their dreams. You could try parking a problem or idea overnight, making sure you keep a notebook and pen or pencil or tape recorder, by your bed. Often, you will find you have the answer in the morning.

(There's a lot of truth in the saying: 'Sleep on it')

Remember Mike Southon's comment? ' Inspiration often happens subliminally. I often have the solutions by morning'

- **Always be ready to receive, and record, the idea. Get to know how best to do this in a way that suits you, and your best 'time' if you have one for this**.

The Inspired Travellers all recorded the inspirations that came to them – but in a variety of ways that best suited them. Ray Cortis draws a plan or mind map (I recommend Tony Buzan's books, 'Use your Head' or 'Make the most of your Mind' or his website for more information about these - find it at www.buzanworld.com - Great for non-linear thinking). Rebekah Renton and Harry Singha keep a note book and jot down ideas, while Keith Hodgson puts his ideas straight onto the computer.

It's a great idea to keep a small notebook by your bed, and another in your wallet, pocket, handbag or briefcase for inspirations while you are on the move – or if you have a Blackberry or Palm pilot, or are comfortable recording into a tape recorder or Walkman/MP3, record the ideas on that. Or you could use a whiteboard (but make sure no one else wipes the ideas off!)

- **Find other inspirational people to be around**

Yes, there are and always will be solitary inspired souls – but most of my interviewees, and I suspect most inspired people, need the company of like-minded others who are on the same wavelength as them at least some of the time, to bounce ideas off, to share thoughts, to listen and question or to have act as Devil's Advocate for their ideas - and to keep them motivated in the 'fallow' times when inspiration feels far away. I recommend that you find or build a community like this (these days it could be a virtual community over the internet though I believe that some direct human contact is always helpful when you feel as if you are ploughing your lonely furrow) - the important thing is the contact and exchange of ideas. Be prepared to give as well as receive,though.

You can find groups of like-minded people all over the place – the Internet is a good place to look - these days there is a wealth of online communities, blogs and sites for every possible discipline - or try your local writers' or artists, or drama group, or your local Chamber Of Commerce or trade/professional groups. You may have to do some searching before you find just the right group of people for you - but the research can be fun.

'Confident Networking' by Gael and Stuart Lindenfield (pub. by Piatkus) is a good book to read to pick up more tips on this.

- **Don't take it for granted**

As with anything really worth having in this world, we have to work at and with inspiration (though the labour can and should be highly enjoyable). Notice how a number of the Inspired Travellers commented that they make a regular practice of seeking inspiration: Nick Williams: 'I am in the habit of immersing myself in inspiration every day'. Ray Cortis: 'When you are centred, you are able to inspire and to be inspired'. Shaun Wallace 'When I pray at night (which I do wherever I am)..' I particularly like what the writer Jack London said about this:

'You can't wait for inspiration. You have to go after it with a club!'

Whether you yourself have a faith and pray or meditate regularly it is a good idea to get into the habit of seeking inspiration in whatever way best suits you. For a lot of people this will involve finding somewhere quiet, peaceful or inspirational (listening to music, or visiting an art gallery) and opening themselves for what happens.

- **Expose yourself to lots of new and different experiences**

Whoever said 'If you carry on doing the same thing, in the same way, you'll get the same results' was inspired! I don't mean that you have to rush off to Paris or the Amazon Rainforest to achieve this (though if you have the means and desire to do so, go ahead with my blessing…) I mean quite simply that you should aim to experience something new, or go about something you already do, in a different way, or look at it in a different light on a regular basis (about every month or so does it for me).

Join that evening class; Step forward and take on that role as secretary or treasurer or president which you were wondering about; read a new magazine or book in a style or with content you would not normally choose ; try making a different dish at home; take a different route to work; challenge some of your own beliefs or try to find out why people who think differently, do so. You will meet different people, learn new things and have new experiences for sure, and these may well lead to inspiration.

Often inspiration is quite simply a different way of looking at something familiar, after all. Very few ideas are completely original; most creative ideas result from combining existing ideas in a new way.

'An idea is nothing more nor less than a new combination of old ideas'

Pareto

In order to grow, we need to challenge ourselves and do things that can be daunting and challenging from time to time.

- **Even when you don't feel inspired – get to work anyway**

Remember Maria Luisa Sanchez La Peña's comment? 'When the muse comes, she must find you working' This is in my opinion the most important point of all.

Even if you don't take action on any of the others, make sure you act on this one.

Researchers have discovered that the subconscious, brain, which governs our impulses and actions, cannot distinguish between what we would call objective reality (what's going on outside the window) and internal reality (what we construct inside our heads). Cognitive therapists have long recommended that people 'act as if' they were experiencing a particular emotion (confidence, success) because behaving 'as if' somehow convinces the subconscious that we really do feel this way. I would call this being in control of our behaviour instead of allowing it to control us. It works just as well with inspiration..if you behave as if you were going to be inspired; sit down in front of your piece of paper, empty screen, lump of clay - and do it regularly enough, slowly but surely, your brain will develop the 'habit' of being inspired. Our inspired travellers have testified to this:

Yvonne Marie: 'I rise to the occasion'

Rebekah Renton:'I choose to get myself into an inspired mood'

Even better, find and use your personal inspiration triggers (music, art, places, people, objects). Trust the process, and stay with it. Sometimes it can be slow and difficult. But as with any habit, once developed and maintained, you will find that it pays off over time. Which brings me to my next point:

- **Persistence pays off!**

All successful and inspired people would agree that simple dogged persistence in the face of setbacks or obstacle is a key part of the route to success – so long as you learn from mistakes.

Thomas Edison held 1,093 patents. He gave himself and his assistants 'idea quotas' because he believed that the more time and effort they put in to searching for new connections and new ideas, the more likely they were to find them, even if some of them didn't work out.

'we have to follow inspiration up with perspiration…we have to work to prove our

faith. Remember that the bee that hangs around the hive never gets any honey'

(Albert E Cliffe)

One of the models I use, which is a favourite of mine, to demonstrate this, is **Kolb's Cycle of Learning**. This shows how most people learn, most of the time.

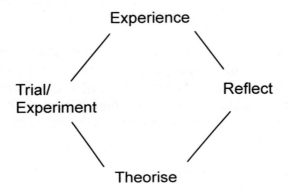

The cycle describes an 'experience' - for example, your first attempt at riding a bicycle. This involves, as those of you who ride bikes will know, not only theory (someone telling you, or you reading about, how to mount the bicycle, get hold of the handlebars, use the brakes and gears etc.,) but 'testing' - at some point, you just have to get on that bike and try to move forward while keeping your balance !

Unless you are an absolute paragon, I imagine that for most of you (and certainly for me) your first experiences of riding a bicycle involved a lot of wobbling and falling off, stopping and starting, and frequent attempts to 'get it right' (experimentation).

Eventually, unless you gave up, you achieved a successful movement forward, pedalling, with both feet off the ground. You now knew and could 'do' the basics of how to ride a bicycle, although complete mastery took longer.

The point of this little example (substitute learning how to cook, drive, read etc etc if you prefer) is that

a) if you wanted or were **motivated** enough to learn the skills and be able to do them, you persisted until you could, and that

b) only hands- or feet- on practice did the trick. It was not enough to **know** about the skills in theory - you had to be able to **apply** them. Only then could you truly say that you could ride a bicycle. And so it is with this journey. You just have to get on the road, and keep going in the face of setbacks. Talking about it from your armchair will not get you to the end of your journey - or even to the start of it.

'A knowledge of the path cannot be substituted for putting one foot in front of the other'

M C Richards

I believe that this is actually very encouraging for anyone who feels they don't have enough 'knowledge'. What you need more than anything else is a willing heart and a sense of purpose.
Don't worry, either, if your first attempts are not perfect. 'The man who never made a mistake, never

made anything', Remember Edison and his 1,039 patents?

You probably won't get it right first time - many people don't. The difference between truly inspired people and the 'hopefuls' lies in the determination to keep going despite the odds.

Another great model for how people learn, which I love and use a lot in my practice to help people to improve their learning skills, is the **'Learning Ladder'**.

THE LEARNING LADDER

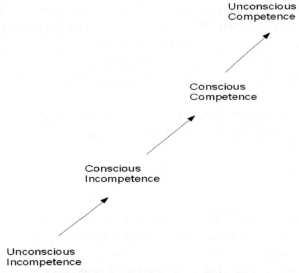

Before you needed to know how to do something, you didn't have the knowledge or the skills, but it

72

didn't matter, because at that point you didn't need them.

Using our metaphor of the journey, you had not yet decided you wanted to set out, or where you were going, so you didn't need to exercise, or learn how to read a map, or find out about the country you were planning to visit. You would have felt quite comfortable being in this state of *'unconscious incompetence'* - (which, by the way, does not mean that you were in a coma, or that you were generally unable to run your life - merely that you didn't have the skills for the next set of tasks you were going to undertake - yet).

Once you do decide that you want to set out on a journey, however, you will be faced with the need to acquire all the skills and knowledge you currently don't have. At the same time, you will realise - and this can be painful - how little you know, and how much you need to learn. It's called *'conscious incompetence'*, and it is not a pleasant or comfortable place to be, but *it has to experienced.*

For most people, in most circumstances, this stage lasts a relatively short time.

The next stage will be *'conscious competence'* where you set about acquiring the skills and knowledge you need, and begin to master them, but still have to make a conscious effort to do so (having to keep looking at the map, and reminding yourself of how the compass works, for example). This stage is clearly more comfortable than the previous one, as you now have the skills or knowledge you need, but you are not yet completely at home with them and you have to make an effort to carry out the tasks involved.

The last stage, *unconscious competence*, is the ideal - at this point you have the skills and knowledge you need, and are carrying out the tasks almost without thinking - they have become second nature, 'part of you', or as described in Neuro-Linguistic Programming, 'in the muscle'. Sometimes this stage is described as 'mastery'.

Like the learning cycle, this model shows that learning never really goes away - we *have* to learn to develop and move on. It also reminds us that the emotions we are likely to experience while learning and going through new experiences will not necessarily always be positive ones. Growth can feel uncomfortable - but we have no choice but to grow. We cannot stay in 'unconscious incompetence' for ever, like the Sleeping Beauty, and remaining in conscious incompetence is painful and stressful and prevents us from being who we were meant to be.

- **Remember to have fun, and do what you love**

If there was one overwhelming characteristic the inspired travellers shared, it was passion for, enthusiasm about, and love of, what they did. Charles Handy, the management organization guru, describes this as 'eudaemonia' or 'flourishing by doing your best at what you are best at'. You should aim to at least enjoy and if at all possible love what you are doing at least 90% of the time – preferably more. Otherwise, why are you wasting your precious God-given time and talents , energy and resources?

What is it that you really love doing and get blown away by? What do you enjoy most in your present job or life? These are good keys to your true inspiration. Generally they are also things you do well.

Passion is the midwife of inspiration. If you can rediscover, or recreate, your true passion, you will surely find inspiration. And everyone has a true passion, no matter what they do or who they are. Some of us have travelled farther away from it than others, but it is still there, waiting to be rediscovered. That is what I mean by 'inspiration is for everyone'.

In the Times Newspaper recently, Ella Stimson asked ten top business people and entrepreneurs what had helped them get to the top of their professions and stay there. Of the ten, no fewer than eight mentioned the importance of passion and loving what they did as key factors in their success – in fact these factors featured more than any other in the careers of very different people. I'll let their words speak for them:

'I don't know anyone who is **passionate** and unsuccessful' (Jean-Pierre Garnier,

CEO, Glaxo Smithkline)

'Enjoy what you do. I'm **passionate** about working with a team on complex

problems'

(Chip Goodyear, CEO BHP Billiton)

'The advice I would give is..whatever you are going to do, if you don't **enjoy** it,

don't do it'

(Philip Green, Owner, BHS and Arcadia)

'Do what you **enjoy** and find satisfying, not what seems to be the fast track or status'

(Val Gooding, CEO BUPA)

'Life is short, and it doesn't make sense if you don't **love** what you are doing'

(Eric Daniels, CEO Lloyds TSB)

'Do what you **enjoy**../.people who have that **enthusiasm** stand out'

(Lloyd Dorfman, CEO, Travelex)

'Don't just go for the money' (Robin Rowland, CEO, Yo! Sushi)

And there's this bonus – if you are doing what you really love and believe in, that belief will carry you through the less good times and doubts. Your heart, as they say, will truly be in the enterprise.

Make the most of your journey (overcoming possible pitfalls and problems)

So far I've talked mainly about the 'upbeat' side of inspiration, and the great feelings you get when inspiration comes to visit or when you have sought it out and found it. However, on any journey, whether a day trip or a long-haul journey, we are bound to encounter some setbacks along the way. It's part of the deal.

The key thing, of course, is how we deal with these pitfalls. We can't always avoid them, but do we just give up, pack up and go home, do we re-evaluate and start again, or do we blame the 'tour operator' or other travellers for our problems? What sort of traveller are **you**?

This questionnaire should give you some clues about your attitude, not only to travel but to new and different experiences in your life. Pick the answer that is closest to your own views or experience.

1 Do you enjoy visiting new places - or do you prefer to revisit places you've been to before?

2 Imagine your friend/partner offers you the chance for a great holiday or trip - but you have to go tomorrow, or at the end of the week. What would be your most likely reaction?

- Fantastic - where are we going?
- It sounds great but what about work, etc.?
- Help - I can't possibly go now!

3 You're held up at the airport. What's your likely reaction?

- Curse, fume, get frustrated
- Get annoyed but then accept the inevitable and try to distract yourself
- Worry and fret
- Keep calm (you must be superhuman!)

4 What's your favourite type of holiday?

- Lap of luxury
- Camping, caravanning or a trek - back to nature
- Casual and laid back
- Cultural
- Hit the nightspots
- Non-stop adventure
- Spa to unwind

5 And, given the choice, who would you prefer to go with?

- Group of good mates
- One or two special friends
- Myself
- Partner
- Family

6 Do you think holidays are:

- Essential
- Help you recharge your batteries
- Refresh you from work or other duties in life
- Nice but not 'real life'
- Bit of a chore

7 Do you travel light, mean to travel light but somehow take more than you intended, or happily take the kitchen sink?

8 What would you not be able to travel without?

- A book or books
- Makeup and other beauty aids or grooming aids if you are a man
- A certain item of clothing
- Your partner or family
- Lots of money/plastic for shopping
- Medical kit
- Your Blackberry or laptop to keep in touch with the office

9 Which of these statements about travelling do you most agree with?

- To travel hopefully is better than to arrive
- There is no moment of delight in any pilgrimage like the beginning of it (Charles Dudley White)
- One's destination is never a place, but a new way of seeing things (Henry Miller)
- Life is either a daring adventure or it is nothing (Helen Keller)

10 Are you glad to get home after your holidays, or do you sometimes wish you could travel all or more of the time?

Of course this is a lighthearted questionnaire aimed at giving you an opportunity to reflect on how you prepare for and experience travel and by analogy other unfamiliar situations. You might like to reflect on some of the answers you gave.

Is there anything you can learn from them?

I've listed here some of the main problems you might encounter in your inspiration journey, and some suggestions and thoughts about how to get over them. I've also included the thoughts and recommendations of the 'inspired travellers' who, of course, encountered their fair share of these problems as well.

'Stuck on the tarmac'

- or, it could be, stuck in dock, or in your driveway. Whichever it is, this one is about getting started. It's understandable - when people are contemplating starting a big, new, project, they may procrastinate - or they may just not be sure exactly what to do first, or to do for the best, to get started.

Here are some tips that might help: pick the ones that suit you and your style

- Planning! Maybe that word strikes terror into your heart. But all journeys benefit from at least a little planning in advance. Planning the main steps you need to take and when you will take them, plus what help and resources you might need, could make all the difference. Some people find a mind map helps; others keep lists or flow charts or prepare a Vision statement to help them get started and keep them on track. Experiment and find out what suits you best.

- Get organized –clear your decks. Find out what works for you to help you forward and put it in place.

- Remind yourself (regularly) why you wanted to set out in the first place! A vision statement can help with this. Keep it where you can see it.

- Use the experience of others who are farther along than you. Has anyone you know done something similar; or could you find someone who has through an organisation or group? If so, talk to them and find out what their experience was like and whether they can save you some time and effort in preparing

- Set a date to start, a date to finish and some milestone dates in between, chart them out, ..and do them!

- Enlist others to encourage you to do these things and check up on you if you have not (a sympathetic colleague, mentor or coach)

- Make it fun/reward yourself when you do achieve (even for small achievements)

- Sometimes you have to just set out in hope…as they say 'the first step is as important…'

Held up

Sometimes, with the best will in the world, things can happen to make your journey longer, more roundabout, or simply delayed for a while. These could be external circumstances, or your own experiences or feelings. This can happen with the best of real journeys, and it can also happen with your inspiration journey, at any point in the journey. So what can you do to mitigate it?

- Expect it, and prepare for it (in your 'contingency' plan above). What will **you** do when something like this happens? (Forewarned is forearmed so think about how you will deal with this should it happen).

- Use the time profitably while you are 'held up'

- Keep on with your useful inspiration habits

- Deal with the bad feelings. Talk to other inspirational people, sympathetic friends, colleagues or a mentor. This is where having a like minded group around you can really pay dividends. It goes without saying that you should expect to do the same for others when they face this predicament.

- Don't punish yourself – all travellers go through this experience at least once…

- Remind yourself of why you began the journey

- Remind yourself of all you have achieved so far (keeping a journal or record can pay dividends here). If you have a vision statement or picture, revisit it to refresh yourself

- Find some inspirational reading, artwork, music or listen to an inspirational CD, depending on your tastes

- Keep the faith, the seeds you have sown will bear fruit (but perhaps not exactly to **your** harvest timetable)

I feel as if I'm climbing a mountain which goes on for ever - will I ever get to the top?

This is a common feeling when people are out on their own and when things get tough, or it's taking longer than they'd planned to reach goals or there seem to be a lot of obstacles in the way. You aren't giving up..but you feel like it! What do you do?

- Remember you are a human being, not a machine or robot. You were made with feelings and emotions as well as thoughts, abilities and a will to act.

- Have faith that if your project is truly what you should be doing, you will get back to it. Your subconscious will most likely be working away without you being aware of it. Remember that farmers often used to let fields lie fallow every few years to regain their richness. You may be experiencing such a period yourself.

- Remind yourself why you started – revisit your vision statement

- Go easy on yourself – if you need to take a break, do something different (go for a walk, practise some sport, look at some refreshing artwork or listen to music – whatever does it for you)

- Nourish yourself with good food, good company, fresh air etc. and ensure you are sleeping sufficiently

Help, I'm lost!

We all can and do go off track sometimes - perhaps just to look at the view and then go back, and sometimes, more seriously, our energies, resources and time can be diverted towards something which is not part of our journey and will not help to get us to our final destination. Sometimes, these activities can be fun and exciting - sometimes, they feel like a duty; sometimes they arise from external circumstances. What can we do when this happens?

- Check that you are actually 'lost' and not just stopping to smell the roses or on an interesting diversion from which you will return in your own time. Your pace and timetable must be your own and governed by you. Being in touch with your feelings will let you know when you need to get back on task .

- Look at what diverts you regularly. Is this something that you can remove from your life? If so, do it! If it isn't (for example, if your family being around is making it difficult to get on with a cherished project – we aren't all like Bach who could apparently work while surrounded by children) plan for space and time when you can take this forward. Book it as a regular appointment in your diary. Ask someone to look after the children for an afternoon. . you can always pay them back with a service of your own. This isn't saying that they are not important – it's merely saying that your project is important to you, too, and deserves to have some time spent on it.

- If you really cannot get away from the diversion at all, forward plan some time when you will be free or freer, and prepare for that time. This will make you feel more in control and put a limit on the 'distraction' which can sometimes seem overwhelming.

Stuck in the middle of nowhere

'Now I saw in my dream, that just as they had ended this talk they drew near to a very miry slough, that was in the midst of the plain; and they, being heedless, did both fall suddenly into the bog...here, they wallowed for a time..and Christian, because of the burden that was on his back, began to sink in the mire' (From 'The Pilgrim's Progress', John Bunyan)

The 'slough' described here is the feeling of frustration and despair at apparently not progressing as fast or as far, or in the exact direction, the traveller had hoped, and running into unexpected difficulties because of this.

However, in the story, while Christian continues to struggle on in the Slough (and eventually gets out) his friend, Pliable, very soon gives up and goes home.

'We can do anything we want, as long as we stick to it long enough'

(Helen Keller)

It's also interesting to note that as well as **persisting** in his own efforts to get out, Christian also gets some **help**.

'He (Help) gave him his hand, and drew him out, and set him upon sound ground..'.

And as well as pulling Christian out, Help points out to him that the solution was literally under his nose all the time and Christian couldn't see it because his **emotions got in the way** .

Help: 'why did you not look for the steps?'
Christian: 'Fear followed me so hard, that I fled the next (nearest) way, and fell in'

So - persistence pays off; don't be too proud to seek and accept help when needed (sometimes someone else will have just the solution you could not see) - and be aware of the possibility that emotion (fear, frustration, anxiety) can literally obscure your view of the obvious.

I'm not sure I can do this...
(or, 'I was sure when I started, but I am not so sure now...)

How we see the world, behave and relate to other people, and what we actually make of ourselves, is influenced by many factors: by our mood at the time, by our experiences, by the people we are with and - crucially - by what we believe about ourselves and our capabilities. If we believe that we are capable of being and, almost more importantly, deserve to be, inspired, then the chances are much greater that inspiration will come when we seek it. If, however, we secretly believe that we are somehow not worthy of this, we will undermine all the good work we've already done and run the risk of not fulfilling our true potential.

So where do all these beliefs come from?

I like to think of the human personality as rather like an iceberg. Only the top 0.1% (approximately) is visible - the rest lurks beneath the surface, endangering passing Titanics.

THE PERSONALITY ICEBERG

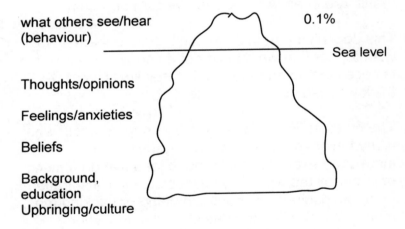

what others see/hear (behaviour)   0.1%

— Sea level

Thoughts/opinions

Feelings/anxieties

Beliefs

Background, education
Upbringing/culture

As the diagram shows, the top 0.1% is made up of the 'visible' aspects of us as human beings - that is, what we say and do. The rest impacts on this - some of it in a more direct way (for example, emotions) - but is not necessarily readily visible to everyone else. Some of it, we don't even know about ourselves! Nevertheless, everything we do and say is affected by the hidden mass beneath the surface.

Our beliefs about ourselves and about other people, and about life in general, are formed very early on by our families, communities and education, and as a result, are often very hard to overturn or modify.

This doesn't mean that we can't change them if we wish to, nor that we should not do so. Sometimes it is necessary to change a belief that limits what we think we can do, for example.

The first step is awareness. Try asking yourself: what is my belief about inspiration in general? An interesting exercise would be to jot down on a piece of paper all the words you associate with 'inspiration' or being inspired - without censoring or thinking too much. Your initial thoughts should reveal your instinctive response -whether this is confusion, mistrust, acceptance or even rejection. Do you believe you can become inspired, or is it something you think is only for other people?

If that is what you think, it's worth spending some time examining why. Our beliefs can be a very powerful motivator to action - but they can also act as a very effective block. We have often held beliefs about ourselves and our capabilities for a very long time, feel comfortable with them, and might have come to see them as reality - that 'that is just how things are'.

Neuro-Linguistic Programming treats beliefs not as truth or facts, but as 'presuppositions' - assumptions we made about the world, or that were made for us, at a time when they were useful and had validity, - but which need to be tested in light of new experience and circumstance.

This is particularly true of our beliefs about ourselves and our capabilities. We might find that, actually, what we thought was true in the past no longer is - we have changed and developed, or the circumstances and other people have changed, so that we need to shift our beliefs or sometimes even overturn them, to accommodate this new reality.

In the *'NLP Workbook'*, Joseph O'Connor writes:

'Have one basic, true belief: You have not yet reached the limit of what you are capable.'

Are you putting a mental ceiling on your own achievements? People are only too ready to own up to what they are 'bad at' than what they are good at, or to tell others what they cannot do. If you find yourself tempted to do this, to say 'I'd like to ....(be able to sing, dance, be manager, get fit, etc) ..but I can't' - stop for a moment to think about why you believe that you can't. Unless your ambition is physically impossible for you, the reason you feel you cannot achieve it is more likely to be inside your own head than external. Adding 'I can't' to your goal effectively turns it into an 'own goal' - tempting you to tell yourself - 'what is the point of trying to achieve it? I'll probably fall flat on my face,'

Worse, if you do pluck up your courage and have a go, and it doesn't quite work out, it can act as a self-fulfilling prophecy - the gremlins get at you and whisper in your ear - 'You see - you were right all along. You can't do it'.

May I suggest that, once you've honestly examined the reasons why you believe you cannot achieve a particular goal, if you find the barriers are family or financial or time based, you add the word 'yet' to your goal statement, and do some serious planning - including timings - to help you get there - and take the first small step. If you find, after asking yourself the question, that there is no valid reason why you can't achieve your goal, find out what the first step you need to take to get you there is (singing lessons? Visiting your local gym?) - and take it. I guarantee that taking action will make you feel so good that you will want to take the next step, and then the next...

Other people think my journey is crazy...

I make no apologies for again quoting from Pilgrim's Progress here:

*' At this, his relations were sore amazed; not for that they believed that what he had said to them was true, but because they thought that some **frenzy distemper** had got into his head..'they also thought to drive away his distemper by harsh and surly carriages to him; sometimes they would **deride**, sometimes they would **chide**, and sometimes they would **quite neglect** him'*

It's a sad fact that, sometimes, other people, even people we love and respect, will not understand our reasons for setting out on a project or dream that is important to us. Worse still, they may actively try to stop us or talk us out of it, as Christian's relatives did - no doubt thinking they had his best interests at heart.

How should we deal with this?

First, a question for you to think about. How would it be if we lived our lives **entirely** by what 'other people' thought? What if the pioneers who opened up the American West had listened to what the pundits said and taken no risks? What if Albert Einstein, Florence Nightingale, Samuel Plimsoll or Martin Luther King (or many other heroes of inspiration) had said to their critics 'You know what?

You're right! Why should I stick my neck out and take these crazy risks, trying to do something that has not been done before, or doing something in a different way? I'll just settle back in my armchair and have a cosy life which conforms to what 'other people' think is the right thing to do' I think you would agree that the world would be a great deal poorer for the loss of their vision and that of many others.

The fact of the matter is that there will always be people who are ready to criticise others for having a vision and the courage to follow it. (Often these are the people who fear taking the first step themselves).

Sometimes the very fact that 'popular wisdom' condemns something makes it all the more viable (in mid Nineteenth-century London, Dr John Snow struggled to convince the authorities that cholera was caused by microbes in water, and not, as current medical wisdom held, by 'bad air'. We all laugh at such a theory now, but at the time intellectuals and prominent people believed this was the case - and thousands died as a result). Your guide must be not what 'other people' think, but what you know and believe in your heart of hearts to be the right course of action for you - and which will lead to a positive outcome.

A few tips which might help if you are facing this problem:

- Know your facts and have them ready. Be very clear why you are taking this course and what the benefits will be for you and others. It's harder to argue against clarity and authority.

- Find people who think and feel as you do to associate with to counterbalance negative nay-sayers

- remember, 'you can tell a man by the company he keeps'

- Consider why people react as they do to someone who has different beliefs or wishes to change. Often, they fear the change, wish they could change themselves, but don't know how, or are afraid that they are going to lose the one they love. Understanding these emotions can help you to deal with them.

- Don't be defensive. You have every right to follow your chosen course, as they have every right not to. They do not have the right, however, to belittle you for persisting in what you want to do.

- Eleanor Roosevelt said: 'No-one can make you feel inferior but yourself' - maybe it is not what other people say, do, or think, but your own beliefs about yourself that hold you back.

'To be nobody-but-yourself in a world which is doing its best, night and day, to make you everybody else, means to fight the hardest battle any human being can fight, and never stop fighting'

e e cummings

I'd like to…but I just don't have the time…

How often have you said to yourself, 'If only I had more time, I'd start that novel, work on that project, contact those people' (insert your own words here)?

When you're busy earning your living and/or keeping a home together, time can seem at a premium. But the fact is, we all do have a certain amount of choice about what we do with our time, and we all do have some free time (even if only a few minutes). How do you spend yours? If you are looking to channel your inspiration, how would it be if you spent a fraction of the time you spend currently watching TV, listening to the radio, or travelling to work, doing just that? Even 15 minutes a day can make a lot of difference over a period of time. It's a question of deciding what is truly important to you, making time for it and doing so consistently - of getting into the habit of it.

Milestones and sights you will see

Travel is, of course, about much, much more than problems and setbacks and uphill climbs. There are many wonderful and exhilarating sights to see and experiences to have along the way. Here are some of the landmarks you might want to look out for and celebrate:

People. You will meet some amazing and inspiring people as you go along your way. This is a guarantee. It will often happen quite unexpectedly. Make sure you build and maintain your networks. Contact with like-minded others, as we've seen already, can sometimes make all the difference between a grim slog and an enjoyable journey.

Places. Could be real places or 'places of the mind'. You will certainly broaden your knowledge of, and deepen your understanding of, the significance of place as you go along your way, seeing them with new eyes.

Experiences. You will most certainly experience new and different things as you go along the way – things which you would never have imagined. And you will be challenging yourself to do things you could only have dreamt of doing.

Why not record these new experiences in a journal?
It will remind you of all that the journey has brought
you , and it will lift you in darker times.

And above all....

what you yourself have achieved (when maybe you
never dreamed you could) There is something
uniquely joyous, satisfying and character building
about stretching and challenging yourself and
achieving what you set out to achieve in pursuit of a
dream – and it goes on to inspire you to greater
achievements. You will find that you just can't sit on
your laurels anymore – you'll be looking out for
how you can make things even better.

**There's a lot to celebrate! Don't lose sight of the
need to celebrate - it's as important to
acknowledge your achievements and take credit
for them, as it is to continue to move forward.**

(How do you like to celebrate? Jot down some
thoughts here - do you like to go out with a group of
friends, or with family, go somewhere or do
something special, or buy yourself a small treat?)

This leads on nicely to the next point.... **enjoying your journey**. Do you remember, at the outset, how I stressed the importance of doing something you are crazy about, that you love, that enthuses you? All the Inspired travellers bore witness to this too.

Imagine that you wanted, really wanted, to go to New York for your holiday. You dreamt of it for months, planned, saved up, got the right clothes and swotted up on the guide books. Yet on the day you somehow ended up in Marbella instead. Now, how would you feel?

Enthusiastic about exploring Marbella and making the most out of the experience? It would be hard work, wouldn't it? You'd feel that you were somehow settling for second best and making the most of a bad job . (This is not to decry Marbella which is a great holiday destination - it's just for comparison).

Would you voluntarily do this on a holiday, which you were supposed to enjoy? So why are you doing this in your life or work? If you are not enthusiastic or at least happy about the situation you are in you are not likely to feel inspired by it. In order to be truly inspired, you need to get more of the 9 out of tens out of your situation. You need to be doing what you really love.

This doesn't mean that you will be walking around with a silly smile on your face 100 % of the time, of course. You will encounter problems and setbacks -

but if you are truly convinced that this is what you really want to be doing and this is where you really want to be, then you are far more likely to overcome them.

Some people have convinced themselves that they are only truly happy when they (and others) subsume themselves in other people's wants and needs. I am not a believer in this. You are a traveller and seeker, not a martyr! Unless helping people is what pushes your particular buttons, that is. This is a question only you can answer, but you need to be totally honest.

So, ask yourself...

What do you really enjoy? It might help to think of a particular time and place and picture it in your mind (draw it if you like doing that). Where were you? What were you doing? Who was there? It's important that you put as much detail in as possible - if you are someone who is inspired by, and who loves, natural beauty, are you going to find your inspiration in an office? (maybe not, or maybe not full time).

Journey's end...or is it?

I prefer to think of this journey as the first of many, or as an entree into a lifetime's journey, because I believe that the inspiration journey, like the journey of self-discovery, never truly 'ends'. Inveterate travellers seem to keep on travelling once they've got the 'bug'. What's more, just as any trip or holiday we take changes us in some way, so embarking on this journey will, I guarantee, change how you see yourself, your world, your chosen career and your relationships forever - in a positive way, of course.

However, it is useful to be able to measure whether you have got to the place you were aiming for when you started out.

How will you know when your journey has 'ended'? In part, it depends where you started from. If your objective was, for example, to find out how others get inspired and to get some of that inspiration for yourself, you may feel that the point at which this was achieved marked the 'end' of that part of the journey - when you sat down and followed some of their examples, or adapted some of their practices for yourself, and found that you too were inspired and able to create something of your own in your chosen field. If this has happened, welcome to a lifetime's exploration as you continue to seek, find and make great use of inspiration for yourself.

Equally, you may find that the objective you had when you started out has changed - I hope, to become more ambitious. Self development can be a bit like that - you climb to what you originally thought was the peak of the mountain only to another, bigger and even more beautiful one behind it!! But the muscles you've developed on the climb carry you on to the next peak of achievement.

I am a great fan of poetry - for me, it epitomises inspiration. That's why I chose the Machado poem to start the book - it sums up how I believe we should approach life. Here's another great poem that seems to sum up that feeling of 'is this really the journey's end, or am I looking for a new challenge now I've overcome that one?' It's by C P Cavafy, the great modern Greek poet, and it's about Ulysses' journey to his homeland Ithaca, after being in Troy for many years, and how the journey has changed him, and how we might experience and make the most of our own personal 'Ithacas'. Enjoy:

Ithaca

"When you set out on your journey to Ithaca,
pray that the road is long,
full of adventure, full of knowledge,
the Lestrygonians and the Cyclops,
the angry Poseidon - do not fear them:
You will never find such as these on your path,
if your thoughts remain lofty, if a fine
emotion touches your spirit and your body.
The Lestrygonians and the Cyclops,
the fierce Poseidon you will never encounter,
if you do not carry them within your soul,
if your soul does not set them up before you.

Pray that the road is long,
That the summer mornings are many, when,
with such pleasure, with such joy
you will enter ports seen for the first time;
stop at Phoenician markets,
and purchase fine merchandise,
mother-of-pearl and coral, amber and ebony,
and sensual perfumes of all kinds,
as many sensual perfumes as you can;
visit many Egyptian cities,
to learn and learn from scholars.

Always keep Ithaca in your mind.
To arrive there is your ultimate goal.
But do not hurry the voyage at all.
It is better to let it last for many years;
and to anchor at the island when you are old,
rich with all you have gained on the way,
not expecting that Ithaca will offer you riches.

Ithaca has given you the beautiful voyage.
Without her you would have never set out on the
road.
She has nothing more to give you.

And if you find her poor, Ithaca has not deceived
you.
Wise as you have become, with so much
experience,
you must have already understood what Ithacas
mean. "

Your souvenirs - what will you bring 'home' with you?

Like any journey, but more so than many in the 'real world', this will change you. You may not bring home a model of the Eiffel tower or a sombrero, but something much more durable: a greater and deeper understanding of yourself and what you are truly capable of, a proper value of yourself as someone who has this capacity to be inspired and to inspire, a sense of wonder at the amazing capacity of the world and the people in it, a set of great, inspirational friends and colleagues, inexhaustible enthusiasm for what you do, improved relationships, as well as tangible achievements in terms of money made, seminars presented, books written, pictures painted, statues carved, photographs taken, hearts mended, others inspired, houses built, terrific businesses set up and run, etc. etc.

- insert here for yourself whatever it is that **you** will inspiringly do and create.

The journey is essentially about learning. That's why so many great works of art have used it as a metaphor (think Pilgrim's Progress, the Divine Comedy, the Odyssey, even the Wizard of Oz) - learning not just about the world out there but about the world inside. These writers and artists understood that reading about and hearing about the journey was not enough however - they wanted to

inspire others, fire them up, to make their own, personal journeys of discovery and to find their own inspiration.

I started this book as a journey in the way we often start them, in hope, but not entirely sure what I would find once I got to my destination. I have found some things I expected to find – the process has strengthened my beliefs that people should do what they love where at all possible, and that there is plenty of inspiration all about us if we look out for it, but I have also received some amazing bonuses along the way, discoveries which I wouldn't have missed for the world. Here are just a few of them:

The most unexpected people and situations can be inspiring and create inspiration;

That there are so many inspired and inspiring people out there;

How fantastically helpful and positive or committed to the project others have been;

How much inspiration is the key to so many aspects of life – this has made the journey even more exciting and profound than I could have dreamt of before I set out;

Last but not least – the book has changed me! While writing it, I have discovered my own wellsprings of inspiration and committed to them anew.

I began writing 'Inspiration: a users' guide' hoping to find common threads which would link inspired and inspiring people. I was not disappointed – there were many common understandings, approaches and attitudes among the group.

However, I also found something I did not expect to find – within these common themes there was wide diversity of approach and emphasis. We are all created, or programmed, with the yearning for inspiration and the capacity to be inspired – how, or whether, we go about this is a matter of individual awareness, choice and preference. We each have to find the path that is right for us and that may be similar or very different to that chosen by others – there is no ultimately 'right' way of achieving this which applies in exactly the same way to everyone.

So if I were in the position of a legislator on inspiration (picking up Shelley's analogy that poets are the 'unacknowledged legislators of the world') I might be able to issue some guidelines or make recommendations, but not lay down rigid rules about what people should do or not do to get inspired. It doesn't work like that!

When I began this book, I set out to show that inspiration is possible for just about anyone in just about any field or occupation, given the right conditions – that inspiration is not reserved for the 'usual suspects' who have the hotline to the muse. Writing the book also showed me that it is not only possible but essential for all of us to be able to access inspiration to live a truly full life. **Your** mission, if you choose to accept it, is to discover what inspiration means for you and to pursue it faithfully and to the best of your own powers, whatever those may be.

'Whatever you can do, or dream you can do, begin it. Boldness has genius, power and magic in it. '

Johann Wolfgang von Goethe.

Happy journeying!

Gill Woon

BOOKS AND WEBSITES I'VE REFERRED TO:

The Beermat Entrepreneur   Mike Southon and Chris West, pub. Pearson Business
C P Cavafy Collected Poems pub. Oxford World Classics
Confident Networking for Career Success and Satisfaction Gael and Stuart Lindenfield, pub. Piatkus
Make the Most of your Mind Tony Buzan pub. Pan Information
Making a Living without a Job Barbara J Winter pub. Bantam Books
The Pilgrim's Progress John Bunyan pub. The Penguin English Library
The Quest of the Overself Paul Brunton pub. Rider Classics
Seeing Spells Achieving Olive Hickmott and Andrew Bendefy pub. MX Publishing
Selected Poems Antonio Machado pub. Harvard University Press
Theory and Practice of the Duende F Garcia Lorca, see Ian Gibson Federico Garcia Lorca, A Life pub. Faber and Faber
Use your Head Tony Buzan pub. Ariel Books
The Work we were Born to do Nick Williams pub. Element

Websites:

www.TrevorBaylisBrands.com

www.buzanworld.com

www.ghanaweb.com

www.seeingspellsachieving.co.uk

www.beermat.biz

www.youthcoachingacademy.com

Also from MX Publishing

Seeing Spells Achieving

The UK's leading NLP book for
learning difficulties including dyslexia

Stop Bedwetting in 7 Days

A simple step-by-step guide to help
children conquer bedwetting problems in
just a few days

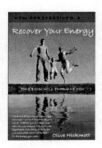

Recover Your Energy

NLP for Chronic Fatigue, ME and
tiredness

More NLP books at www.mxpublishing.co.uk

Also from MX Publishing

Play Magic Golf

How to use self-hypnosis, meditation, Zen, universal laws, quantum energy, and the latest psychological and NLP techniques to be a better golfer

Psychobabble

A straight forward, plain English guide to the benefits of NLP

You Too Can Do Health

Improve Your Health and Wellbeing, Through the Inspiration of One Person's Journey of Self-development and Self-awareness Using NLP, energy and the Secret Law of Attraction

More NLP books at www.mxpublishing.co.uk

Also from MX Publishing

Process and Prosper

Inspiring and motivational book from necrotising faciitis survivor Wendy Harrington. Amazing book for anyone facing critical trauma.

Bangers and Mash

Battling throat cancer with the help of an NLP coach. Keith's story has led to changes in procedure in many cancer hospitals and is an inspiration to cancer patients everywhere.

Performance Strategies for Musicians

Tackle stage fright and performance anxiety using NLP. David has worked with some of the worlds leading classical and rock musicians and leading businesspeople to help them perform in public

More NLP books at www.mxpublishing.co.uk

Lightning Source UK Ltd.
Milton Keynes UK
21 November 2010

163233UK00001B/36/P